A Greener Printer

Dale Stubbart

Books by Dale Stubbart are
Like the Flight of the Swallow
Uplifting the Heart

Engaging
Well-Written
Easy to Read
Light
Decent
Different
Humorous

A Greener Printer
For Personal Use and
Small Businesses

Rated: G
Reading Level: 6th Grade Easy

Longest Word: Congratulations

A Greener Printer

**For Personal Use and
Small Businesses**

Contents

A Greener Printer

For Personal Use and Small Businesses

A Greener Printer

For Personal Use and Small Businesses

A Lesson from Grandmother

My Grandmother would send my parents hand-written letters from time to time.

She would start on the front of a sheet of paper. When that was filled, she would continue on the back of the paper. When that was filled, she would return to the front of the paper. There, she would fill the top margin. Then she would fill the right-hand margin (turning the paper sideways). Next came the bottom margin. And finally, she filled the left margin.

Then she'd turn the paper over again and fill the margins on the back side. When she had completely run out of room; that was the end of her letter. Grandmother had been an

A Greener Printer

For Personal Use and Small Businesses

English Teacher for many years and an Editor at a Newspaper for many more. So, her letters never ended awkwardly in the middle of a sentence.

I thought it was humorous for her to do that rather than use another sheet of paper. Now, I do the same thing in order to save paper, in order to save trees, in order to save the environment.

Grandmother grew up in a time when paper was a luxury. It was not something to be wasted.

Now, in order to reverse climate change and restore the natural ecosystem, I'd rather see trees planted, than see them cut down, especially if it's just for paper.

Grandmother learned how to use the internet and send email. But, I think she only did that for work. I on the other hand use the internet and email for both work and

A Greener Printer

For Personal Use and
Small Businesses

pleasure. This helps cut down on my paper usage.

Here's to you Grandmother, for teaching me how to save paper!

A Greener Printer

For Personal Use and Small Businesses

Introduction

So, what does that story about Grandmother have to do with a greener printer?

There are three things that make a printer green: the paper; the energy used; and the ink. I'll address those things in that order, more or less.

The easiest way to make your paper usage greener is to use less paper. For printing, this can be done with double-sided or duplex printing. It can also be done by printing on smaller sheets of paper. Or you can go all out by using tree-free paper.

A Greener Printer

For Personal Use and Small Businesses

Greening your energy usage consists mostly of using a low energy printer. Look for Energy Star or some other energy efficiency label.

Printers usually need to be left plugged in, even when they're not in use. While they're plugged in they use some energy from time to time.

Greening your ink is perhaps the hardest part. Less toxic inks are available, but they usually require a specialized printer.

I'll explore all that in detail in this book.

A Greener Printer

For Personal Use and Small Businesses

Other Ways to Save Paper

Another method of saving paper is to use junior size legal pads. If most of your writing consists of notes, and your notes do not usually take more than that size sheet of paper (5 in by 8 in), this will save paper. You can turn it over for another set of notes.

Better yet, use a regular sheet of paper folded in half horizontally. That way, you have two smaller sheets of paper (when turned sideways). Using a sheet of paper that's already been printed on one side works, but only if the print isn't dense enough to make it hard to take / read your notes.

A Greener Printer

For Personal Use and Small Businesses

Some people save paper by buying lined (ruled) paper with thinner lines. Narrow ruled paper has 1/4 in lines. Medium (College) ruled paper has lines which are just a hair wider. Wide (Legal) ruled paper has lines which are almost 3/8 in wide. Junior Legal Pads come in Narrow and Medium ruled. This method doesn't work so well for me as I tend to write outside the lines. It's an old habit from my childhood days when I tended to color outside the lines. Come to think of it, I still do that.

You can make your own paper out of many things, even broccoli. Most recipes include recycling newspapers or scraps of other paper. And you probably have plenty of paper that you're recycling. Basically, you can use anything that's fibrous which your blender can shred, to make paper. This includes egg cartons, leaves, flowers, grass clippings, clothing scraps.

A Greener Printer

For Personal Use and Small Businesses

If you want your paper to have a lighter color, soak your shredded mixture in hydrogen peroxide. Otherwise, you might have to buy some pens with white ink.

Making hand-made paper takes lots of patience and time. But if you want to do something fun and artistic and craftsy, try making your own paper.

You can make your own kit or buy one. There are plenty of recipes on the internet. Though most of them use perfectly good sheets of paper to make hand-made paper. And that would defeat the purpose of saving paper.

You probably won't be able to set up something to produce paper which will feed into your printer.

When Grandmother grew up she had to peel potatoes. Then she had to peel the

A Greener Printer

For Personal Use and
Small Businesses

potato peels to make sure that they got every last bit of potato. Too bad she didn't know she could have made paper out of those peels.

A Greener Printer

For Personal Use and Small Businesses

Updating Grandmother's Lesson

I don't write much by hand – and you should be grateful. There are times when even I can't read my own handwriting. Especially, if it's been a while since I wrote it. Most of my writing is done on the computer. Occasionally, I print it out for others to read.

Perhaps the simplest methods of saving paper and printer ink, are presented by Print Greener and Change the Margins.

A Greener Printer

For Personal Use and Small Businesses

Print Greener sells GreenPrint Software. That software intercepts what you're printing on your computer before it reaches the printer. It allows you to specify which pages to not print.

Print Greener also sells the Evergreen Font. That font spaces letters closer together. This saves paper and ink, by printing more in less space.

You may or may not be able to buy anything from Print Greener. The font was free for a while, then not. Now, it seems Print Greener is selling its software and fonts through printer companies. My last printer came with the software already installed.

Change the Margins is a campaign which encourages you to reduce your word processing default margins to three-quarter (.75) inch. Of course, you can reduce them

A Greener Printer

For Personal Use and Small Businesses

even more (depending on your printer and if you want page headers and/or footers).

I recommend changing the margins to one-quarter (.25) inch, if your printer allows that. In this book, I've chosen one-half (.5) inch margins. That way, the printing doesn't get lost in the edge of the book. I could do one-half inch margin on the edges which will be bound and one-quarter inch margin on the other edges. But, that's too much work.

Change the Margins also has a petition to ask Microsoft to change the defaults to three-quarter inch.

A Greener Printer

For Personal Use and Small Businesses

Additional Changes to the Way you Print

These are additional changes you can make to the way you print to save paper:

You can make changes to your Word Processing App / Program to make your printer always print in duplex (double-sided) mode when possible. You can do that provided your printer prints in duplex reliably. Or you can print one page at a time and manually duplex the printout.

You can print two pages per page and duplex at the same time. That will give you four pages per printed page. Of course you

A Greener Printer

For Personal Use and Small Businesses

might need to buy new glasses if you do that.

Choose a low ink use font. Sans serif means that the letters don't have tic marks. See the **Heading**. For sans serif fonts choose Evergreen or Arial Narrow first, then Arial, then Verdana, then Tahoma, until you get the look you want.

Serif fonts, such as Times New Roman, often use shorter letters then sans serif letters. So, you get a few more lines on a page. However the serifs (tic marks) take more ink to print them. So, I'm not sure that serif saves any ink.

And of course every bigger font, bold and underscore takes more ink. Italic text might ink, if it skews the letters enough to make them take more room than normal.

All the fancy script fonts take more ink. Still, you don't want to make your print too dull and boring.

A Greener Printer

For Personal Use and Small Businesses

Make your Website Save Paper and Ink

Web page programmers can make their web pages use less paper and ink when a user prints their webpage. This can be done by offering a print link to a separate page without graphics and minimal text. Alternatively, you can do this in the background via the CSS Media=Print option. (CSS is the styling language for websites.)

A Greener Printer

For Personal Use and Small Businesses

Theoretically, you can condense the font-spacing also. Nevertheless, that takes a lot of programming. And it usually doesn't work.

Perhaps the easiest thing to do in this regard, is specify fonts in CSS with more condensed font-spacing as the first choices. Rather than condensing the font-spacing, you can just reduce the font-size when printing.

If you design fonts, consider designing a condensed one which uses less ink.

Change the foreground color of the print version of your website to black or perhaps gray. Black ink is typically less toxic than colored ink.

Set some sections of your website to not print. These might include images, portions of menus, etc.

A Greener Printer

For Personal Use and
Small Businesses

Print lower resolution versions of images.

Set the background color of your website to transparent when printing.

Reduce the margins.

I explain all this in my book <u>Designing your Website to Use Less Energy</u>.

A Greener Printer

For Personal Use and Small Businesses

Change how Webpages Print

Internet Explorer allows you to change how pages print. In my version, I click on Settings (the gear). Then, I click on Printer, then on Page Setup. There, I can enable Shrink-to-Fit (default), change the Margins, and change the Font.

Firefox allows me to change the font, but not specifically for printing. If I click on Developer in Settings, I can change the style by going to the Style Editor. Google Search results page has 17 stylesheets – which one do I change? And where do I change it? And, it looks like none of those is specifically for printing.

A Greener Printer

For Personal Use and Small Businesses

With Chrome, I may be able to change some settings when printing the page, depending on the printer. Under Advanced Settings, I can change the font and/or font size.

I don't know anybody who does this. They probably don't do it because it's a lot of work. And it may not always work. It's dependent on the printer, the browser, and the webpage.

There are a couple of websites – PrintFriendly.com and PrintWhatYouLike.com which claim to allow you to do this easily. You can try them at your own risk if you want.

The simplest thing to do is to allow the webpages to print as they want to. If you want to employ a little extra work, you can

A Greener Printer

For Personal Use and Small Businesses

hold down the Alt Key while pressing the PrintScreen Key. (On my laptop I also have to hold the Func (Function) key). That copies the current screen. Then paste that into a Word Processor, modify, and print.

Perhaps it's easiest to just hold down the Ctrl Key and press p. This will bring up the Print Dialog in any web browser. Then click on Properties. Here, you can usually select duplex printing.

A Greener Printer

For Personal Use and Small Businesses

Tree-Free and Tree-Friendly Paper

For those of us, who still need to print a lot or still need a lot of paper to write on, there's tree-free and tree-friendly paper. We already discussed that you can make your own paper. Yet, that paper probably won't work in your printer. There are places where you can buy various types of handmade paper. Some of those will work in your printer. Some won't.

I've switched to buying only tree-free and/or tree-friendly paper for printing. Here's what's available, that works in my

A Greener Printer

For Personal Use and Small Businesses

printer. 100% PCW (Post-Consumer-Waste) paper and Bagasse (Sugar Cane) paper are similarly priced to regular printer paper. The rest run more, depending on content and availability. Only 100% PCW and 100% Hemp are available in both Letter (8.5in x 11in) and Legal (8.5in x 14in) sizes.

I define tree-friendly paper as 100% PCW, or made from part of the tree (bark, prunings, etc.) and the tree was allowed to continue to live.

I don't consider PCW at less than 100% to be tree-friendly, even if the paper is made from multiple ingredients, the rest of which are tree-friendly or tree-free. Post-Consumer-Waste mainly means that it was made from stuff you put out in your recycling bin. So, it already had one use and has now been processed again for a second use. And hopefully, you'll recycle it again.

A Greener Printer

For Personal Use and Small Businesses

The opposite of Post-Consumer-Waste is Virgin. A tree was cut down and directly used for the first time in this product. The opposite might be Post-Industrial-Waste. In this case, the tree was made into lumber or something else (perhaps paper). Post-Industrial-Waste is what was left over from that process.

Bagasse is French for Pulp. Specifically, it's Sugar Cane pulp. Most Bagasse comes from Brazil where it is used to make paper. They also turn it into electricity. In Brazil, Bagasse is Bagaço.

U.S. paper sizes are Letter, Legal, Executive, and Parent Sheet. Letter is 8.5in x 11in and works in most printers. Legal is 8.5in x 14in and works in many printers. Executive size paper can be cut to give you two Letter-size pages or almost Letter-size pages. You can get Executive Sheets cut at

A Greener Printer

For Personal Use and Small Businesses

most Office Supply stores and at your local printer. Parent Sheets can be cut into six Letter-size sheets at your local printer. Office Supply stores usually don't have the equipment to cut Parent Sheets.

Some paper supply companies will cut larger sheets to Letter-size for you. The rate they charge for this is usually less than having it done at your local printer, but more than having it done at an Office Supply Store.

Tree-free and tree-friendly papers might be available in International Sizes (A4, A6, B4, B6, C4, C6 etc.), but not in US.

Tree-free and tree-friendly mailing envelopes are available, usually in #10 Envelopes. #10 is the regular envelope used for mailing letters. #9 is the slightly smaller return envelope.

A quire is 25 sheets of paper. A ream is 20 quires or 500 sheets. A bundle is 2 reams or

A Greener Printer

For Personal Use and Small Businesses

1000 sheets. A bale is 5 bundles or 5000 sheets.

Those measurements may still be used in some places. However, you'll only be dealing with sheet, ream, and case which is 12 reams. A case is equivalent to 3000 sheets. (Each ream is wrapped separately inside the case.) You can remember the other measurements for trivia and Scrabble.

In the table below PCW refers to 100% PCW unless specified otherwise. Hemp / PCW refers to Hemp mixed with PCW. Bagasse / Bamboo / PCW refers to Bagasse mixed with Bamboo mixed with PCW. Etc.

These papers were available when I made this table in 2015. As time passes, it seems that fewer and fewer options are available for tree-free and tree-friendly paper. You may want to buy a case at a time to ensure that you have plenty while it's available. If

A Greener Printer

For Personal Use and Small Businesses

you do that, do not store it in too damp of an environment.

100% PCW, Bagasse, Cotton, and Hemp are probably here to stay. I use 100% PCW or Bagasse for normal printing. Lokta has been around for a while. It is my favorite for when I want a textured paper or something that's a little thicker.

Paper Content	Useable in Printer	Comments
Amate	No	Nicely patterned craft paper made from bark – Mayan craft. Used to back paintings.
Bagasse	Yes – works just like regular paper.	Variations: 100% Bagasse; Bagasse / Bamboo / PCW; Bagasse / Hemp / Linen. Mixed Cardstock available. #10 Envelopes available.
Bamboo	Yes – nicely crisp	Comes in Parent Sheet

A Greener Printer

For Personal Use and Small Businesses

Paper Content	Useable in Printer	Comments
Banana Leaf	Yes - Yellow	100% Banana Leaf and mixed with PCW. Mixed is also available in Executive size. Mixed Cardstock available. #10 Envelopes available.
Coffee	Yes – Brown	Mixed with PCW #10 Envelopes available.
Cork	No – glued backing heats up and mucks up the printer.	Nice for scrap book covers or covering fishing poles.

A Greener Printer

For Personal Use and Small Businesses

Paper Content	Useable in Printer	Comments
100% Cotton	Yes	Various weights are available. If it's not 100% Cotton, it's usually mixed with less than 100% PCW so doesn't qualify. Cotton, unless Organic is harvested by killing it with pesticides. I did find one source of Organic Cotton paper, but they were going out of stock. So, 100% Cotton qualifies, but you may not want to use it. Cardstock available. #10 Envelopes available.
Denim	Too heavy – light Blue	Made from recycled jeans no doubt #10 Envelopes available.
Garlic	No	Garlic / Lavender is also available.
100% Hemp	Yes – works just like regular paper. Has a light Tan shade.	The Declaration of Independence was written on Hemp Paper. Available in Letter and Legal sizes. Hemp / PCW is also available in Letter. Cardstock available. #10 Envelopes available.

A Greener Printer

For Personal Use and Small Businesses

Paper Content	Useable in Printer	Comments
Mulberry (Kozo, Saa)	No – Mottled color or too light-weight.	Tree-Friendly as made from bark
Lokta	Yes – rough texture, lighter Tan than hemp, sort of a Cream. Weight varies by sheet.	Lokta is an evergreen shrub which grows in Nepal. Every year, they prune it to the ground, every year it grows back 4 ft. They clear it to grow food. Cardstock available. #10 Envelopes available.
Mango Leaf	Yes – nice orange shade	Banana, Coffee, Mango, and Lemon papers are usually mixed with other agricultural waste and PCW. Also available in Executive size.
Lemon Leaf	Yes – light Yellow shade	Also available in Executive size.

A Greener Printer

For Personal Use and Small Businesses

Paper Content	Useable in Printer	Comments
Papyrus	No – Woven, stiff	"The Original Paper" – at least one of the originals – Rice and Bark are others.
Poo (Dung)	Supposedly – I haven't tried it. One-sided only as ink seeps through.	Available in Cow, Horse, and Elephant varieties. Sometimes mixed with other agricultural waste. Elephant Dung Cardstock available. #10 Envelopes available.
100% Post-Consumer-Waste (PCW)	Yes – works just like regular paper.	Available in Letter and Legal sizes. Cardstock available. #10 Envelopes available.
Rice (Unyru)	Questionable – may be too heavy	Various varieties, mostly handmade
100% Straw	Tan shade, haven't tried it.	There is also Straw cardstock available. However, it is only mixed with 30% PCW. So, it doesn't qualify.

A Greener Printer

For Personal Use and Small Businesses

#10 Envelopes are also available in Cigar paper and Kenaf. Kenaf is related to Hibiscus. It looks like a very tall grass – 11 ft tall. Kenaf paper was popular in 1990's, but has been discontinued.

If possible, buy a sample of paper to try in your printer before ordering a lot. Check your printer specs before purchasing. Papers come in various weights – lbs or gsm. Depending on what type of paper you're buying – regular, cardstock, etc., the same weight will mean different things.

I purchase paper from Green Earth Office Supply, Green Line, and Neenah. I purchase 100% PCW from Office Depot. However, it's only available online, not in the stores.

Dick Blick is great for the craft papers. The ones listed above don't work in my printer.

A Greener Printer

For Personal Use and Small Businesses

I Buy Southworth paper from Office Depot online. It's 100% Cotton.

Reich Paper is another good company. Their cardstock runs a little thick for my printer specs. However, it still works. I don't want to use that cardstock too often. That's OK. They also have paper.

I buy Hemp paper from Rawganique. That's a great company which sells all sorts of Hemp clothing and other products. Unfortunately, there's a $30 fee because it's being shipped from Canada.

Green Field sells Denim paper. They also sell paper which has seeds planted in it.

Other suppliers I haven't tried include Colors of Nature, Dwellsmart, Hemptopia, Ellie Pooh, PooPoo. I met one of the founders of Ellie Pooh. He seemed like a great guy.

There is a water-proof paper for sale on the internet. It's being promoted as tree-free.

A Greener Printer

For Personal Use and Small Businesses

Well, it is tree-free. Nevertheless, as near as I can tell, the main ingredient is petroleum. So, that disqualifies it.

A Greener Printer

For Personal Use and Small Businesses

Green Printing Companies

You can buy your own green printer or you can outsource your printing (send it off) to a Green Printing Company.

If you outsource it to a Green Printing Company, you'll usually need to have a lot of copies of something printed, at least 100 sheets. 500 sheets or more will make the cost more reasonable. Having 10,000 business cards printed at a time will get you a good price. (That's about 800 sheets of paper.)

So, who are the green printing companies you can outsource your work to?

A Greener Printer

For Personal Use and Small Businesses

Greener Printer is perhaps the greenest – 5 stars.

Hot Cards has the most locations. So, delivery is probably the shortest distance and therefore the greenest – 5 stars.

Printing for Less – 5 stars.

South Bay Press is a local green printer in Lacey, WA.

Seattle Garment and **BCI** are green clothing label printers in Seattle.

Print my Thing prints labels for clothes, jars, candy, etc., etc.

Others include:
- **Gemini Print Group**
- **Zoo Printing**.

A Greener Printer

For Personal Use and Small Businesses

Green Printers

In my book (that's a pun), green printers are those which can print on tree-friendly paper. They are also need to use little energy and non-toxic ink.

Since tree-friendly paper is very similar to regular paper, all printers qualify on that particular point. Tree-friendly cardstock sometimes runs heavier than 80lb. Heavier also means thicker. Most printers bend the paper / cardstock as it goes through the printer. For 80lb cardstock and lighter, that is not an issue – it will bend back automatically. Heavier cardstock is best printed on printers which do not bend the paper while printing. These are specialty printers. They're probably outside of your price range, unless you're setting up a

A Greener Printer

For Personal Use and Small Businesses

printing company. Also, 80lb is over the specs for what most printers will print.

Green Printers use little energy. Most, if not all printers sold in the US have Energy Star ratings. That's good, but doesn't narrow the field. The Energy Star website only tells you that a printer is rated as passing. It doesn't tell you exactly what that rating is.

The website does however, offer these tips for buying a green printer:

=> Look at power used in sleep mode and automatic shut off.

=> Look for automatic duplex (double-sided) printing. Yes, you can do manual duplexing, but will you? Even if a printer offers automatic duplexing, it probably does not offer it for heavier cardstock (over 40 lbs).

=> Look for various quality settings. You probably won't use them for draft copies. Still, they're good to have in case you might.

A Greener Printer

For Personal Use and Small Businesses

Typically, inkjet printers have one cartridge for black and one for all the other colors combined. If any one color runs out you have to replace the color cartridge. Look for a printer which has separate color cartridges. Start with Epson.

Some printers combine colors when printing black. They might do that, even though they may have a separate cartridge for black ink. Since black ink is typically less toxic than colored ink, you may want to look for a printer which uses black ink to print black. This will also save you money, as black ink is less expensive than colored ink.

You might also consider whether the printer is just a printer, or if it is also a scanner and copier. Alternately, you can buy a separate scanner for less than $100. Then

A Greener Printer

For Personal Use and Small Businesses

you can scan in what you want to copy and print it out. If you have a digital camera or cell phone, you can take a picture of what you want to copy with that. You can transfer that picture to your laptop. Then, you can print it out for your copy. It may not be the best copy. Still, in many cases it will do.

But perhaps the major consideration for buying a printer is quality. Brands available at Office Depot include Brother, Canon, Dell, Epson, HP, Lexmark, OKI, Panasonic, Ricoh, Samsung, and Xerox.

In my opinion, the better quality brands are Canon, Dell, Epson, HP, Panasonic, Ricoh, Samsung, and Xerox. That's 163 printers to choose between. (I assume you want a color printer and that you want to spend less than $1000).

If you limit those printers to 5 and 4 star rated ones, that's still 134 printers to choose between.

A Greener Printer

For Personal Use and Small Businesses

Please turn to the next page to see how you can limit your choices even further.

A Greener Printer

For Personal Use and Small Businesses

Narrowing the List

For personal and small business printers, you are basically limited to laser printers, ink-jet printers, and solid ink printers. 3-D printers typically melt plastic. So, they're out.

Laser Printers use toxic chemicals to dry the ink. So, even if they use non-toxic ink, they're out. Congratulations, you're down to 89 choices!

Color Ink Jet printer cartridges come in two varieties – single color and multiple color. Ink Jet printer cartridges also come in two varieties – those with the print head imbedded in the cartridge and those without. Embedding the print head in the cartridge,

A Greener Printer

For Personal Use and Small Businesses

rather than having it in the printer seems wasteful to me. So, HP is out. Epson and Cannon do not have the print head in the cartridge. I'm not sure about the others.

The print head is that little metal thing which figures out how to print various characters. IBM Selectric Typewriters allowed you to change the print heads for various fonts. Now, I'm aging myself.

Eliminating HP took about 40 printers out of the running. So you've only got about 50 printers to research. 50 printers is not that many when you realize that you will probably eliminate a lot more once you start. You'll probably start to eliminate them, depending on how they look, how much money you want to spend, and what you're favorite brand is.

A Greener Printer

For Personal Use and Small Businesses

Next, I'll cover your options for non-toxic ink. That will really narrow down your list of choices.

A Greener Printer

For Personal Use and Small Businesses

Non-Toxic Ink

Your choices for non-toxic ink are very limited.

Inkpal sells Soy Ink Laser Cartridges. If you choose to use a laser printer, they probably have a cartridge which will fit it. Soy Ink is less toxic than petroleum ink. Nevertheless, it may still have drying agents. And those are the most toxic part of the ink, when it comes to printing.

Green Planet also sells soy ink laser cartridges mostly for HP printers.

ColorCon sells inkjet cartridges containing non-toxic ink for some printers.

Epson, Canon, HP and others sell Ink Tank Printers. These printers come with a

A Greener Printer

For Personal Use and Small Businesses

built-in tank which holds about two-years-worth of ink. When the ink runs low, you refill the tank. You'll have to make sure that you can refill the tank with a non-toxic ink. Also check to make sure that the non-toxic ink won't mess up your printer.

Don't buy in to an ink refill schedule when you buy your printer. Those refills will contain toxic ink.

Two years of toxic ink, then perhaps forever of non-toxic ink.

Soy and Vegetable Ink for refilling tanks is much easier to come by than Soy and Vegetable Ink Cartridges.

Xerox made Solid Ink Printers. The ColorQube Office Printer uses ink crayons which are non-toxic. Perhaps you can find one of these printers used.

No word on how much longer Xerox will keep making the ink crayons. The crayons are shaped so that you can only put the

A Greener Printer

For Personal Use and Small Businesses

proper color in the proper slot on the proper model of printer.

Some of Xerox's Office Laser Printers may now use a similar non-toxic ink, in a laser cartridge. Their safety sheet says the ingredients in the ink are paraffin wax, resin, and pigment. The wax should dry without any drying agents. So perhaps this is non-toxic.

There are also Edible Food Inks mostly sold by InkEdibles. These work in some Epson, Canon, Brother, and CakePro printers. It's not clear that the inks work for current models of these printers.

Edible food ink is made mainly for printing food labels. Not sure if it would work for other types of printing.

And those are your choices as far as non-toxic inks are concerned.

A Greener Printer

For Personal Use and
Small Businesses

You can check California regulations on various inks. Their standards for non-toxicity are stricter than most states. They are also more strict than those of the federal government.

A Greener Printer

For Personal Use and Small Businesses

Conclusion

I bought a Xerox ColorQube while they were available. The Solid Ink Crayons are still available. Xerox suggests I upgrade to the Versalink. If the time ever comes that I need to replace my printer, I'll check out all of my options then.

I really like the ColorQube. And the ink is truly non-toxic.

Solid Tank printers intrigue me. However, I'm not sure that I can wait two years to use up the toxic ink.

I also only buy tree-free or tree-friendly paper. Mostly I buy 100% Post-Consumer Recycled Paper or Sugar Cane Paper. I can save money and it's more readily available

A Greener Printer

For Personal Use and Small Businesses

if I buy a case at a time. I also really like Lokta paper when I want a paper with more texture.

Since I have a non-toxic printer, and I use tree-free or tree-friendly paper, and since I only print a few business cards or brochures at a time, I don't have a need for a green printing company.

I design my websites to save ink and paper. I also design them to use less energy. You can read more about that in my book <u>Designing your Website to use Less Energy</u>.

And for most things I print, I set the margins to .25 inches all around.

I publish my books with print on demand publishers. This saves paper by printing a book only when somebody purchases it.

A Greener Printer

For Personal Use and Small Businesses

I tried to print books myself and sell them. However, I ran into issues with getting them bound, and with selling them. So I let the self-publishing company do the printing and selling for me.

Those are my conclusions. Your conclusions may be different.

Hopefully you can use this book as a guideline to help you make your decision when you purchase A Green Printer.

A Greener Printer

For Personal Use and Small Businesses

Updated Conclusion

We moved from Washington State to Hawaii. My Xerox ColorQube weighed a lot. But, it was coming with us. There was just one little snag.

Our house in Washington sold before we could secure a place to live in Hawaii. So, we put our stuff in storage in Washington. Then, we took a detour through Minnesota for personal reasons.

It was supposed to be a sixth month detour. However, when we found out that it was going to be much longer, I went back to Washington to ship some of our belongings

A Greener Printer

For Personal Use and Small Businesses

to us. During that trip, I found out that our movers had placed the printer on its head [the front of the printer was facing down], even though I had correctly labeled **UP** on the box.

Three years later, when that printer arrived in Hawaii, it was again standing on its head. Excitedly, I tested printing a page. But, the rollers which feed the paper wouldn't budge.

That may have been due to the printer standing on its head. That may have been due to it sitting for three years without being used. Whatever the case, I needed a new printer.

At first, I tried to just print at UPS. But, then, the number of pages that I was printing, made that cost too great.

A Greener Printer

For Personal Use and Small Businesses

I checked again for the most eco-friendly printer. Xerox no longer sold the ColorQube, nor anything similar. So, I reinvestigated EcoTank Printers. Those turned out to be the least toxic Printers that I could find.

I had two concerns

- How toxic was the ink?
- How toxic was the drying agent?

I somehow managed to get ahold of someone at Epson who told me that the ink in their EcoTank printers was very non-toxic. I believed him. He also said that there was no drying agent. That part seemed a little questionable but not unreasonable. These Epson EcoTank Printers are inkjet, rather than laser. So, they wouldn't need as much drying agent.

When the printer arrived, I found out in the literature, that these Epson EcoTank Printers don't heat up in order to dry the ink.

A Greener Printer

For Personal Use and Small Businesses

That explained why no drying agent was needed.

I've had my new printer for over one year. There's still enough black ink left for at least another year. In addition to the black ink tank, there are also separate tanks for three colors. Since I mostly print black and gray, all of those are almost full.

When my black ink runs out, will I buy more Epson ink or will I go with a soy-based ink? At this point, I don't know. But, like the person at Epson said, their ink is very non-toxic. So, I'll probably go with a proven product, unless I have a good reason to do otherwise.

On a side note: I will probably run out of paper before I run out of ink. I ran out of paper once and ordered a couple of reams of tree-free paper. Both reams were torn when

A Greener Printer

For Personal Use and Small Businesses

they arrived – that happens to lots of packages here. Still, most of the paper was usable.

For a while, I wasn't using hardly any paper. So, I gave lots of it away.

Now, I'm printing more. But, it will still be a few months before I order more paper.

I'm putting that off for as long as I can, hoping that I can find a way to the paper shipped here without losing 50 or so sheets.

Those sheets may not be usable in a printer. But, I will still be able to use them to take notes. So, they won't really be lost.

A Greener Printer

For Personal Use and Small Businesses

Who Wrote This Anyway?

Dale Stubbart and his wife live in *Paradise*. They live there, providing that they haven't forgotten for the moment where that is or what that's like. We try to allow ourselves to be happy and not get bogged down by fear.

I was headed down the road to *Misery*, rather than the one to *Paradise*. However, something went awry. And I kept being reminded of who I was and where I belonged. When I'm back in *Paradise*, I can help others recall what's really important.

A Greener Printer

For Personal Use and Small Businesses

I help others Transition their Dreams and Visions. I walk with people into the dream state where fairies, angels, bumblebees, whatever, help bring their dreams to life. I draw on my experience with Spirit, Earth, Stories, and IT to help people transform their lives and thus the world.

The Writing Muse found a willing partner in me for 90+ Titles. I can help you get your book self-published too. As an Author, I write stories in many genres or categories. Often my stories include several genres. *Romance* often accompanies *Fantasy*. And one of my books is a *Western Sci-Fi*.

You'll find humor and romance in many of my books. I keep them clean, non-formulaic, and happy. Many of my books include poetry. Sometimes I include phrases and words from languages other than English. Yet they're still easy to read, even my reference books.

A Greener Printer

For Personal Use and Small Businesses

My books are far from boring, as my narrators and others have confirmed. To help in that regard, I keep my books concise, yet complete. As my wife says, I'm the only person she knows who can write a novel in a page. That may be a slight exaggeration.

I write stories I like to read. You'll find yourself right smack dab in the midst of the story. And you'll have an enjoyable journey all the way through.

All of my books are on my website – Stubbart.com. The search box works very well.

My *Spiritual* books include Spiritual Reference, Mystical Writings, Spiritual Fiction, and Fiction with a Spiritual Theme. I write these with my self=friend *Yellow Bear.*

My *Earthwise* books include books for Living with Multiple Chemical Sensitivities,

A Greener Printer

For Personal Use and Small Businesses

Energy-Wise Transportation, and others to help you live your Earthwise lifestyle.

My *Computer* books are written to be easily understood, even if you have limited technical experience. In fact, about 1/2 of them are non-technical in nature, especially my book about a Robot who falls in love.

My *Reference* books are informative. They are stories, not just data, facts, and figures. Delve into your preferred topic or choose to learn about something new. My *Reference* books include books on *Food*.

I write Romance because I'm truly in love, just ask my wife. My *Romance* stories will speak to the true Romantic in you, the one who wants to love and be loved.

Children are some of my favorite people, no matter how old they are. My *Children's* stories will speak to the child in you. Let that happy baby come alive!

With Fantasies anything can happen and in my *Fantasy* stories it often does. Cheer

A Greener Printer

For Personal Use and Small Businesses

on these protagonists as they live their unimaginably real lives in their impossibly real worlds. Get surprised with delight.

Fiction allows me to write what could happen. My *Fiction* stories allow you to consider alternate possible outcomes. What would the world be like, if ...?

Outer Space, Aliens, Science Fiction intrigues me. These *Sci-Fi* stories will speak to the space-farer and voyager in you. New worlds are out there for you to discover.

I write Thrillers when I no longer want to run and hide. My *Horror*s will help you face your fears. Franklin Roosevelt said, "The only thing we have to fear is fear itself." At times, it can scare the $#@! out of me!

There are basically two ways to get to Paradise. You can enter by facing your fears and pains and allow them to dissolve and be healed. Or you can enter through joy and beauty. You can rest assured that I will enter through joy and beauty 99 times out of 100.

A Greener Printer

For Personal Use and Small Businesses

And when you're willing, I'll take you with me. *Paradise is waiting for you. What are you waiting for?*

So take a trip on over to Stubbart.com. Find out more about my books and my work with Dreams. With over 90 books, I'm certain you'll find something to your liking. Or my name's not *Dale Stubbart*.

Dale & Terry Stubbart

www.ingramcontent.com/pod-product-compliance
Lightning Source LLC
Chambersburg PA
CBHW070857070326
40690CB00009B/1882